The Honeybee Sisters Cookbook

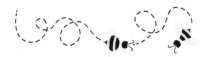

Dedication

To my mom, Anne Gappmayer, who taught her six daughters the
homemaking arts and gave us a priceless lifetime gift.

—JB

To my best friend and husband of thirty-one years, Brent Daines,
who has never once complained about our food bill.

—TD

To Travis. I'm sorry, babe, that there is only one recipe in here with peanut butter.
Maybe Jennifer can write a sequel: *The Peanut Butter Brothers*. Love you!

—AJ

ISBN 978-0-9976993-0-2

All food styling and photography by Tearsa Daines, Alicia Johnson, and Jennifer Beckstrand

Book and cover design by Kim Coxey

Text and photographs © 2016 Jennifer Beckstrand

Published July 2016 by Jennifer Beckstrand Publishing

 # Foreword

My idea for the Honeybee Sisters series was born on a beautiful September day on an Amish farm in northern Wisconsin. The Wisconsin Amish farmhouse, complete with buggy, barn, and a plethora of chrysanthemums, was the ideal setting for three charming Amish love stories. I loved the idea of a trio of sisters who kept bees and lived with their eccentric aunt Bitsy. Immediately after the idea took hold, I started dreaming of all the wonderful honey recipes that could be part of the Honeybee Sisters series. What could be more fun than for the Amish sisters to make tasty honey recipes that entice the boys to come to Honeybee Farm?

Since it is against their religion to be photographed, this cookbook is my imagining of what the Honeybee sisters' world is like, with no offense meant to anyone, including my many Amish friends. The girls in the photos—Meg Daines, Lauren Henrie, and Emma Daines Smith—are sisters, but they are not Amish, though they had great fun dressing Plain. I could not have completed this project without them or without the incredible culinary talents of my dear friend Tearsa Daines and the stunning photos by multi-talented Alicia Johnson.

Be sure to check out the back of this cookbook for a sneak peek of *Sweet as Honey*, the first book in the Honeybee Sisters series, in which Aendi Bitsy points her shotgun at poor Dan Kanagy. You don't want to miss it. And don't miss other delicious recipes and quilting advice posted monthly on my blog at jenniferbeckstrand.com.

I hope you enjoy the tasty world of the Honeybee Sisters! I have certainly enjoyed creating it for you.

Jennifer Beckstrand

 # Introduction

When my girls told me they wanted to write a cookbook, I wasn't too keen on the idea. Food attracts boys like honey attracts bees. I warned them that if they didn't want the boys hanging around the house, they shouldn't make the cakes and pies and cookies that are sure to bring them running. My nieces didn't seem to be alarmed about the prospect of boys all over the place, so I suppose they'll have to learn the hard way.

My problem is that smart, feisty, pretty girls attract boys even better than honey does. So even if my girls stopped cooking altogether, I have a sneaking suspicion that the boys would still find excuses to come over.

Some of the recipes in this book, like Honey Glazed Pretzels and Whole Wheat Bread, are very traditional Amish dishes. Others, like Salmon Tacos and Coconut Lime Chicken, are less traditional but still *wunderbarr*. I lived as an *Englischer* for twenty years before coming back to the Amish to raise my three nieces, and as a dental hygienist, I collected a lot of recipes.

Here's my final warning: Boys are like stray cats. If you feed them, they'll keep coming back. Use this cookbook at your own risk.

Aendi Bitsy

Table of Contents

Main Dishes

Teriyaki Flank Steak and Honey Sweet Potatoes

2–4 pounds flank steak

Marinade

½ cup low sodium soy sauce
4 tablespoons burgundy cooking wine
1 tablespoon apple cider vinegar
1 clove garlic, pressed or minced
2 teaspoon ginger, minced
1 tablespoon honey

Score flank steak by gently cutting shallow diagonal lines on both directions of the flank steak. Do not cut deep into the meat. Repeat on other side of the steak.

Combine all marinade ingredients into a gallon zipper plastic bag. Add steak and shake gently to mix. Marinate steak overnight or at least 4 hours, turning halfway through.

Grill over medium heat approximately 7 minutes per side, basting with marinade as you grill.

Remove from heat and tent with foil for 5–7 minutes. Slice thinly across the grain.

You can heat the remaining marinade in a pan on the stove and pour over sliced meat or you can serve on the side.

Serves 4–6.

Honey Crashed Sweet Potatoes

Poke holes in 3 medium sweet potatoes with a fork. Wrap in foil and roast in 350° oven 60–70 minutes or until tender. Unwrap and let cool. Increase oven temperature to 450°.

Combine in a saucepan:
1 teaspoon crushed red pepper flakes
¼ cup honey
4 tablespoons unsalted butter

Bring to a simmer on low, stirring occasionally to combine. Remove from heat and add 2 tablespoons apple cider vinegar.

Smash potatoes with the palm of your hand, then tear or slice into thick slices. Toss in a large bowl with half the honey mixture. Arrange skin side down on unlined baking sheet and bake until browned around the edges, 20–25 minutes. Drizzle with remaining honey mixture.

Luke didn't need more convincing. For as enthusiastically as he ate, he was probably starving all the time.

Salmon Tacos with Pineapple Salsa

Salmon Tacos
1 salmon fillet (about 1½ pounds)
12 corn tortillas
½ cup fresh squeezed lime juice
Zest of 2 limes
¼ cup extra virgin olive oil
¼ cup honey
3 cloves of garlic, pressed
½ teaspoon kosher salt
Shredded Monterey Jack cheese
Cilantro sprigs and lime wedges

Salsa
¼ of a pineapple, peeled, cored, and chopped
2 tablespoons red pepper, finely chopped
1 tablespoon cilantro, chopped
1 green onion, finely chopped

Prepare salsa by mixing all ingredients together. Cover and refrigerate.

Heat each corn tortilla directly on stove burner a few seconds per side. Wrap in foil and keep warm in a 175° oven.

In a small bowl, whisk the lime juice and lime zest, olive oil, honey, and garlic together. Reserve 2 tablespoons of the marinade and pour remainder into a gallon plastic zipper bag. Add salmon fillet and marinate for at least one hour but no longer than 3 hours. Heat grill on medium-high heat and grill salmon for 5 minutes per side or until thickest part of fillet flakes easily with a fork or internal temperature is at least 145°. You can also bake at 350° for 12–14 minutes. Remove from heat and sprinkle with salt. Flake with a fork and add reserved marinade. Divide among tortillas. Add cheese and pineapple salsa and garnish with cilantro sprigs and lime wedges.

Makes 12 tacos.

Aunt Bitsy grunted. "That boy is so crazy for Poppy, he'd eat sawdust if she fried it up."

Beef and Green Bean Stir-fry

1 ½ pound flank steak, sliced very thin against the grain
½ cup low sodium soy sauce
3 tablespoons sherry or cooking sherry
2 tablespoons honey
2 tablespoons cornstarch
1 tablespoon ginger, peeled and minced
8 ounces green beans, ends trimmed and cut in half
4 whole scallions, cut in half-inch pieces diagonally
3 tablespoons olive oil
Red pepper flakes

In a bowl, mix together soy sauce, sherry, honey, cornstarch, and ginger. Reserve half the liquid and pour the other half over the sliced meat. Set aside.

Heat oil in a heavy skillet or wok over high heat. Add green beans and stir for 1–2 minutes or until tender crisp. Remove to a separate plate. Set aside.

To the heated pan, add half the meat mixture, spreading it out as you add it. Top it with half the scallions, leaving most of the marinade in the bowl. Do not stir the meat for at least a minute. You want it to brown as quickly as possible. Turn meat to the other side, not stirring, and cook for another 30 seconds. Remove to a clean plate.

Repeat with other half of meat, first allowing pan to get very hot. After turning the meat, add the first plateful of meat, the remaining marinade, the rest of the scallions, and the green beans. Stir to combine over high heat for 30 seconds. Turn off heat. Mixture will thicken as it sits.

Sprinkle with red pepper flakes and serve with jasmine rice.

Serves 6.

Bee's Knees Corn Dogs

4 cups canola oil
3 cups Krusteaz pancake mix
1 cup cornmeal
1 ½ cups water
1 egg, slightly beaten
½ cup honey
12 bun-length beef hot dogs, cut in half
24 6-inch lollipop sticks

Preheat canola oil in a deep, heavy pot on medium low. Heating gradually helps maintain a steady temperature. Heat to 375°, adjusting heat to hold temperature. In a deep bowl, whisk dry ingredients together. Add water, egg, and honey. Mix together with rubber spatula until mostly smooth. The batter will be quite thick and should hold its shape when you run your finger down the center. If it's too thin, the batter won't stick to the hot dog. You can easily adjust by adding more water or more pancake mix until you get the right consistency.

Push the lollipop stick about two-thirds of the way into the hot dog. Dip into batter, covering completely. Carefully set into hot oil, turning with tongs until the batter starts to brown. Don't let the corn dog touch the bottom of the pot. (It should stay buoyant.) You may add up to 3 corn dogs to the pot, but add one at a time and make sure they start to develop a crust before you add more. Continue turning so the corn dogs brown evenly. Cook until the corn dog is a deep golden brown. Remove and drain onto paper towels. For an extra touch of sweetness, drizzle a small amount of honey over the corn dog and serve with mustard.

If you want to use the extra batter, you can thin with milk or water and use for pancakes or you can drop teaspoons of batter into the hot oil and brown like a donut hole. Roll in cinnamon and sugar or powdered sugar immediately after removing from oil.

Serves 24.

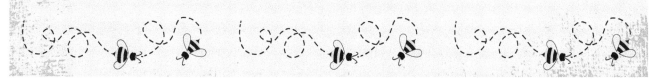

Sweet and Spicy Pork Roast

1 pork tenderloin
1 Golden Delicious apple, peeled, cored, and thinly sliced

Rub
1 teaspoon salt
¼ teaspoon pepper
½ teaspoon ground cumin
½ teaspoon chili powder
½ teaspoon cinnamon

Combine rub ingredients in a small bowl and rub pork loin with the mixture. Heat
1 tablespoon of olive oil in a heavy skillet and brown the roast on all sides. Remove from
heat and transfer to a roasting pan or shallow baking sheet, arranging sliced apple around
the tenderloin.

Combine in a small bowl
¼ cup dark brown sugar
¼ cup honey
1 tablespoon minced garlic
½ tablespoon Tabasco sauce

Pat this mixture on top of tenderloin. Bake at 350° for about 25 minutes or until internal
temperature is 145°. Remove from oven and let stand for about 10 minutes, tented with foil.
Roast will continue to bake while tented. Slice and arrange on platter, spooning apples
around the roast. Drizzle with any remaining drippings.

Serves 4.

Sticky Wings, 2 Ways

Sesame Sticky Wings

4 pounds chicken wings, cut at joints and discard wing tip
1 large garlic clove, minced
1 teaspoon salt
2 tablespoons soy sauce
2 tablespoons hoisin sauce
2 tablespoons honey
1 teaspoon Asian sesame oil
Pinch of cayenne or dash of Sriracha
1 ½ tablespoons sesame seeds, lightly toasted
1 scallion, finely chopped

Heat oven to 425°. Line a large shallow baking pan with foil and spray with non- stick cooking spray. Combine garlic, salt, soy sauce, hoisin sauce, honey, sesame oil, and cayenne or Sriracha and toss with prepared wings. Spread wings on the prepared baking pan in one layer and drizzle with any remaining sauce. Roast, turning over once, until cooked through, about 35 minutes on each side. Remove immediately to platter and drizzle again with any remaining sauce. Top with scallion and sesame seeds.

Spicy Honey Wings

Prepare 4 pounds of wings as above and sprinkle generously with seasoning salt such as Lawry's. Spray a baking sheet with non-stick spray and spread wings onto the baking sheet. Bake at 375° until golden brown, 1 ½ –2 hours. They should have the appearance of being deep-fried but don't let them brown too much or they will dry out.

When wings are almost done, warm ½ cup honey in small saucepan on stove and whisk in 1 tablespoon of apple cider vinegar. Brush onto wings the final minutes of cooking. Remove wings from pan onto platter. Drizzle with the remaining sauce.

Serves 6–8, allowing 4–6 wings per person.

Coconut Lime Chicken With Coconut Rice

2 pounds boneless, skinless chicken breasts
3 tablespoons olive oil
Zest and juice of 1 lime
1 teaspoon ground cumin
1 ½ teaspoons ground coriander
2 tablespoons low-sodium soy sauce
2 tablespoons honey
2 teaspoons curry powder
½ cup coconut milk, light or regular
Pinch of cayenne pepper
Chopped cilantro and lime wedges for garnish

Prepare chicken by rinsing and patting dry. If the chicken breasts are thick, butterfly them so the marinade can permeate the meat.

In a gallon size zipper plastic bag, combine olive oil, lime zest and juice, cumin, coriander, soy sauce, honey, curry powder, coconut milk, and cayenne pepper. Close bag and shake gently to combine. Add chicken breasts and marinate 2–8 hours, turning them halfway through.

Preheat grill or grill pan to medium high heat. Grill breasts 6–7 minutes on each side. (They will need less time if you butterflied the chicken.) While meat is grilling, pour the remaining marinade in a small saucepan and bring to a boil. Boil 5–10 minutes, stirring occasionally.

Remove from grill and drizzle with sauce and sprinkle with cilantro. Serve with lime wedges and coconut rice.

Coconut Rice

1 cup jasmine rice
1 cup coconut milk, light or regular
1 cup water
½ teaspoon salt

In a medium saucepan, bring all ingredients to a gentle boil. Cover and reduce heat to low and simmer 15 minutes or until most of the liquid evaporates. Remove from heat and let sit an additional 10 minutes. Fluff with a fork and serve.

Serves 4–6.

Rose very nearly turned and ran up the stairs and fled to the safety of her room, but that would leave Luke to spread the dressing on the pizza, and he wasn't even good at pouring water.

Killer Bee Pizza

Basic Dough
2 cups warm water
2 tablespoons olive oil
2 tablespoons honey
1 tablespoon Saf instant yeast
1 ½ teaspoons salt
4–5 cups flour

In a large mixing bowl, add 2 cups warm water, honey, and yeast and let yeast bloom. Add salt and olive oil and 3 cups of flour and mix. Continue adding flour, ½ cup at a time, until dough pulls away from the sides of the bowl. The more flour you add, the thicker the crust. We like a thin crust so I add flour just until the dough is slightly sticky to the touch. Then when rolling out, I roll in about ¼ cup more flour. Let dough rest for 10 minutes and divide into 3 equal pieces. This will make 3 pizzas, or 2 pizzas and one calzone. Roll out or shape dough and top with desired sauce and toppings. Bake on preheated pizza stone, lightly greased cast iron skillet, or cookie sheet at 475° or grill on high 8–10 minutes.

Killer Bee Pizza
Skin or peel 6–8 cloves of garlic and place on a small piece of tin foil. Drizzle with olive oil and seal closed. Bake at 350° for 15 minutes.

When garlic is roasted, put in a garlic press or mince then spread evenly on pizza dough along with the remaining olive oil. Top with 1 ½ cups mozzarella cheese and 6–8 slices of sopressata or dry salami that has been sliced into long thin strips. Add chopped or sliced tomatoes. Sprinkle lightly with chili oil. Bake at 475° for 8–10 minutes.

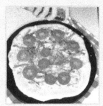

Remove from oven and drizzle lightly with honey.

Bitsy rolled her eyes at the ball of fur that turned out to be a fat kitty. "She's not much of a security system. Doesn't make a peep at trespassers and wouldn't attack a robber even if he had a slice of bacon wrapped around his neck."

Barbecue Chicken Thighs

2–3 pounds boneless, skinless chicken thighs

Barbecue Sauce
1 ½ cups ketchup
¼ cup Worcestershire sauce
½ cup brown sugar
½ cup honey
½ cup red wine vinegar
2 ½ tablespoons dry mustard
2 teaspoons smoked paprika
2 teaspoons Tabasco sauce
2 teaspoons salt
1 ½ teaspoons black pepper
½ cup water

Whisk sauce ingredients together and refrigerate until ready to use.

Rinse chicken thighs well and pat dry. Trim thighs of additional fat and put in a gallon zipper plastic bag. Reserve 1 cup of the barbecue sauce and pour remaining sauce over the chicken thighs. Marinate overnight or for at least 8 hours.

Grill over medium heat about 10 minutes per side or internal temperature is 170°, basting with sauce from the zipper bag. Remove from heat and drizzle with 1 cup reserved sauce. Cover loosely with foil until ready to serve.

Serves 6.

Salads

Asian Potluck Slaw

Salad
½ head green cabbage, shredded
½ head red cabbage, shredded
½ cup slivered or sliced almonds, toasted
2 green onions, sliced
2 tablespoons sesame seeds, toasted
1–2 packages of ramen noodles, broken up
2 cups shredded chicken (optional. If making
as an accompaniment dish, omit chicken.)

Dressing
3 tablespoons honey
¾ cup vegetable oil
1 tablespoon sesame oil
⅓ cup plus 2 tablespoons rice
wine vinegar
2 flavor packets from chicken or oriental
flavor ramen soup
½ teaspoon pepper

For dressing, combine all dressing ingredients and mix well.

Mix all salad ingredients together and toss with half of the dressing. If making ahead of time, add the noodles, almonds, and dressing just before serving. Taste and add more dressing as needed.

For color and another layer of flavor, add 1 can of drained mandarin oranges.

Serves 8–10.

Strawberry Spinach Salad with Honey Raspberry Dressing

1 pound spinach
5–6 strips of bacon, cooked and crumbled
¼ cup red onion, sliced
½ cup parmesan cheese, shredded
¾ cup slivered almonds, toasted
2 cups strawberries, quartered
10–12 wonton wraps, cut into strips and deep-fried until golden brown

Combine all ingredients except wonton strips. Just before serving, add wonton strips and toss with dressing.

Serves 8–10.

Raspberry Honey Dressing

½ cup red wine vinegar
½ teaspoon dry mustard
1 teaspoon salt
½ cup raspberry jam
⅓ cup honey
¾ cup canola or vegetable oil

Combine all ingredients except the oil and shake or whisk well. Slowly add oil while whisking or blend in blender to combine.

"Did you know it takes two million flowers to make one pound of honey?" Rose said. Josiah widened his eyes. "I should plant more roses."

Salad De Maisson

2 hearts of Romaine lettuce, or 1 large head of Romaine, washed and chopped
4 ounce bag of slivered almonds, toasted
¾ cup parmesan cheese, shredded
1 cup Swiss cheese, grated
1 pound bacon, cooked and chopped (optional)
1 ½ cups croutons

Combine all ingredients and toss with about one third of the dressing. This is our favorite salad! We always double the dressing recipe so we always have it on hand. Refrigerate remaining dressing.

You can also add 2 cups grape tomatoes or 1 cup grilled, chopped chicken breast for a main course salad.

We like homemade croutons for this salad. Start by slicing bread into ½ inch cubes. (Day old French bread or ciabatta bread are our favorites.) Toss 4 cups of cubes with 2 tablespoons olive oil and sprinkle with 1 teaspoon each salt and pepper. Toss again to coat evenly. Spread on cookie sheet and bake at 400°, 10–12 minutes or until lightly toasted. Let cool completely and guard/hide until ready to serve.

Serves 8–10.

Dressing
Juice from 1 lemon
3 cloves of garlic, crushed
1 teaspoon salt
½ teaspoon pepper
¾ cup canola oil
1 tablespoon honey

Combine lemon juice, garlic, salt, and pepper. Slowly whisk in oil until combined. Refrigerated 1–2 hours before serving. Discard garlic before using.

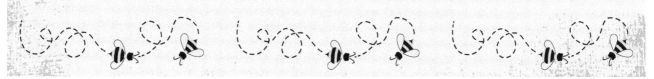

Thai Noodle Pasta Salad

3 Filet Mignon steaks
1 4-ounce package of Chinese egg noodles, cooked per
package directions, drained, and cooled
12 cherry tomatoes, cut in half
8 baby carrots, julienned
½ cucumber, peeled, seeded, and julienned
1 ½ cups Napa cabbage, shredded
2 mangos, cut into chunks
10 large basil leaves and 10 mint leaves, chiffonaded*
2 tablespoons chopped cilantro
3 green onions, thinly sliced
1 cup salted peanuts, chopped

Grill, broil, or pan sear the steak 2–3 minutes on each side or to desired doneness. Remove from heat and tent with foil to keep warm. Toss the noodles with ¼ cup of the dressing. Add the rest of the ingredients except for the peanuts. Add more dressing to taste. Cut steak into half-inch chunks and add to salad. Toss and divide into 4 large main dish portions or 8 side dish portions. Sprinkle with chopped peanuts and serve.

*To chiffonade basil and mint, stack the leaves on top of each other. Roll them up together in a long tube then use a sharp knife to slice across them into thin ribbons.

Dressing
¼ cup fish sauce
½ cup sugar
¼ cup honey
2 teaspoons minced garlic
½ cup Sambal Oelek
½ cup lime juice
1 cup peanut oil
1 tablespoon sesame oil

Combine all ingredients, except the oils and whisk together. Slowly whisk in oil in steady stream and whisk to combine. *It is important not to use a blender with the Sambal Oelek. The seeds will release heat and make the dressing too spicy.

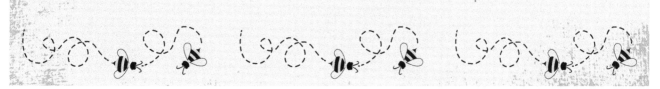

Breads

Whole Wheat Bread

2 ½ cups hot tap water
½ tablespoon salt
1 tablespoon gluten flour
2 tablespoons vegetable or canola oil
½ cup honey
5–6 cups fresh ground whole wheat flour
1 tablespoon Saf instant yeast

In a large bowl or bread mixer, add water, salt, gluten, oil, honey, and half of the flour. Mix until combined and then add the yeast. Add the remaining flour just until the dough comes away from the sides of the bowl, being careful not to add too much flour. Let machine knead an additional 6 minutes. If kneading by hand, add 2 additional cups of flour and combine in bowl and then turn out onto floured surface and continue to knead in flour until it no longer sticks to your hand and is soft and satiny. Let rise 10–15 minutes in the bowl. With oil on your hands, divide dough into 3 equal pieces, shape into loaves, and place in medium-sized loaf pan. Let rise again for 10–15 minutes and bake at 350° for 30 minutes. Remove from oven and turn pans onto their sides and rest for 10 minutes. Turn bread out of pans.

This is a good all purpose dough for rolls or hamburger buns, etc.

Makes 3 medium or 2 large loaves.

Cornbread
1 cup butter or margarine, softened
½ cup honey
3 eggs, slightly beaten
3 cups Bisquick baking mix
5 tablespoons corn meal
¾ teaspoon baking powder
½ teaspoon salt
1 ½ cups milk

Preheat oven to 350°.

Cream butter with honey. Add eggs and mix. Add remaining ingredients and mix well. Batter can be slightly lumpy.

Pour into a greased 9X13 pan and bake for 40 minutes. Serve with honey butter.

Honey Butter
1 cup butter, softened
1 cup honey
1 egg yolk
½ teaspoon vanilla

Combine all ingredients and whip until fluffy. Make sure to refrigerate because of the egg. You may omit the egg yolk. It just won't be as fluffy.

Serves 12.

Brown Sugar and Honey Muffins

½ cup butter
½ cup brown sugar
½ cup honey
1 egg
1 teaspoon vanilla
1 cup milk
2 cup flour
1 teaspoon baking soda
½ teaspoon salt

Preheat over to 350°. Cream butter, brown sugar, honey, egg, and vanilla together. Add remaining ingredients and mix with wooden spoon until smooth. Fill greased muffin tins two-thirds full and sprinkle brown sugar over the top of each muffin. Bake for 18–20 minutes. Remove from oven, let rest 5 minutes, and then loosen and remove from tin.

Makes 12 muffins.

"I could eat nothing
but a whole plate of rolls
and be quite content."

Beehive Crescent Rolls

2 cups hot water
⅓ cup honey
⅓ cup butter, softened
2 ½ teaspoons salt
⅔ cup powdered milk
5–6 cups flour
1 egg
2 tablespoons Saf instant yeast

In a large bowl, combine first 5 ingredients along with 2 cups of flour and mix until smooth. Add yeast and egg and combine. Add 2 more cups of flour and then add additional flour, ½ cup at a time until dough pulls away from side of bowl or if kneading, until it no longer sticks to your hands and is smooth and satiny. Be careful not to add too much flour or the rolls will be heavy. Place dough in a greased bowl and grease the top of the dough lightly. Cover tightly with plastic wrap and let rise until triple in bulk. Punch down and let rest for 5 minutes.

Divide into 3 equal pieces. Roll out one piece of dough into a circle and spread with softened butter. Cut with a pizza cutter into 8 wedges, like you would a pizza. Starting at the wide side, roll to the center and then shape like a crescent on a greased baking sheet. Repeat with the other 2 sections of dough. Let rise for about 30 minutes. Bake in at 375° for 15-20 minutes or until the tops are golden brown. Remove from oven and brush tops with melted butter.

Makes 24 crescent rolls.

Poppy might be feisty, but she knew how to use a hammer and how to cook. Luke would brave a hundred of her scowls for a loaf of that bread. He'd put up with three lectures for a plate of honey pecan sticky rolls.

Honey Pecan Sticky Rolls

Rolls
See page 43 for basic roll dough recipe.

Filling
¼ cup butter, softened
¾ cup honey
1 cup pecan halves
⅔ cup sugar
2 teaspoons cinnamon

Grease 2 muffin tins and at the bottom of each place ½ teaspoon butter, ½ tablespoon honey, and 3 pecan halves. Divide dough into 2 sections and roll each section out in a rectangle. Mix ⅔ cup sugar and 2 teaspoons cinnamon together. Spread dough with softened butter and sprinkle with cinnamon and sugar mixture. Roll the long side of the dough up like a jelly roll and cut with string or knife into 1 inch slices. Place in prepared muffin tins and let rise until double in bulk. Bake at 375° for 20 minutes. Remove from oven and immediately turn out onto large platter.

Makes 24 sticky rolls.

Honey Glazed Pretzels

Dough
2 ½ cups all-purpose flour
½ teaspoon salt
1 tablespoon honey
2 ¼ teaspoon Saf instant yeast
1 cup warm water

Topping
½ cup warm water
2 tablespoons baking soda
Coarse salt (optional)
2 tablespoons each butter and honey melted together, or 3 tablespoons butter, melted.

Mix the water, honey, and yeast in a large bowl or mixer. Wait 5 minutes for the yeast to bloom. Add salt and 2 cups flour and mix until smooth. Add ¼ cup more flour at a time and knead until dough pulls away from the sides and bottom of the bowl. Turn on to a work surface and continue to knead the dough for about 5 minutes, until it is soft and smooth. The dough shouldn't be sticky but shouldn't be tough either. Spray a plastic bag with cooking spray and place the dough inside the bag and seal. Let rise 30–60 minutes.

Preheat oven to 500° (Yes! 500°) and line a jelly roll pan with parchment paper.
Divide dough into 8 equal pieces and let rest for about 5 minutes. Combine baking soda and very warm water and place in a shallow bowl and stir until dissolved. Roll the dough into ropes, about 12 inch long, and twist into the shape of a pretzel. Dip pretzel in water and baking soda. (You will have to stir the water/soda mixture each time to keep it from separating.) Place pretzels on the baking sheet and sprinkle with sea salt or coarse salt. Let rise for 10 minutes.

Bake the pretzels for 7 to 9 minutes or until they're golden brown. While baking, melt the honey and butter together, if desired.

Remove the pretzels from the oven and brush or drizzle with the honey butter or butter. Best when eaten warm!

Makes 8 pretzels.

Treats

Honey Bee Lemon Pound Cake

Cake
1 ⅔ cups all purpose flour
½ teaspoon baking soda
½ teaspoon baking powder
3 large eggs
½ cup sugar
½ cup honey
2 tablespoons salted butter, softened
1 teaspoon pure vanilla extract
1 teaspoon pure lemon extract
Juice from two medium lemons (approximately ⅓ cup)
½ cup vegetable oil

Icing
1 cup powdered sugar
1 ½ tablespoons whole milk
½ teaspoon pure lemon extract
Zest from ½ of a lemon

Preheat oven to 350°.

Grease a 9x5 loaf pan well.

Zest half of one lemon and set aside.

In a medium bowl, mix flour, baking soda, and baking powder.

In mixing bowl or stand mixer, cream butter. Add sugar, honey, eggs, vanilla, lemon extract, lemon juice, and oil until mixed well. Add dry ingredients and blend until smooth. Do not over mix. Pour batter into prepared pan and bake for 45–50 minutes or until toothpick comes out clean. Edges should be a dark golden brown. Let the pan sit for at least 10 minutes on its side, and then flip over on to cooling rack. Let cake cool before icing.

For icing, blend powdered sugar, milk, and lemon extract until creamy. Ice the top of your cake and let the icing drip down the sides. Sprinkle with lemon zest. Let icing set before slicing. You can also make as cupcakes or individual bundt cakes. Reduce baking time to 20–25 minutes or until a toothpick inserted comes out clean.

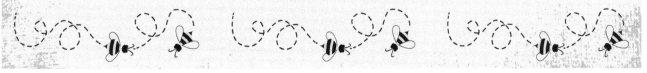

Pear Honey Crumble

1 ¼ cup flour
1 cup rolled oats
1 cup packed brown sugar
1 teaspoon cinnamon
½ cup butter, melted
3 medium pears, peeled and sliced
¼ cup honey
¼ cup butter

Preheat oven to 350°.

In a small bowl, combine flour, oats, brown sugar, cinnamon, and melted butter, and mix until crumbly. Set aside 1 cup of mixture and press the rest into an 8-inch square baking dish. Arrange pears over crust.

Over low heat, melt ¼ cup butter and ¼ cup honey together. Pour over pears. Sprinkle with reserved crumb mixture.

Bake for 30–35 minutes or until top is golden and bubbly around the edges. Serve warm with whipped cream or ice cream. Sprinkle with nutmeg, if desired.

Serves 9.

Sweet and Salty Honey Coconut Granola

2 ½ cups rolled oats (not quick)
2 cups sweetened coconut
½ cup whole raw almonds, coarsely chopped
½ cup macadamia nuts, coarsely chopped
1 teaspoon cinnamon
1 teaspoon salt
⅓ cup honey
⅓ cup extra virgin olive oil
½ teaspoon vanilla

Preheat oven to 325°. Combine all dry ingredients and mix well. Combine honey, olive oil, and vanilla. Pour over dry ingredients and mix well. Spread on a large cookie sheet either sprayed with non-stick cooking spray or lined with parchment paper. Bake 10 minutes and stir gently. Bake additional 10 minutes until golden brown. Let cool, then break into pieces. Store in an airtight container.

Makes 6 cups.

Nutella Calzone

Basic Dough
See page 25 for basic dough recipe.

Nutella Calzone
Shape or roll dough into a thin circle and place on pizza stone or cookie sheet. Spread half the dough generously with Nutella, being careful not to spread right to the edge. (Be generous with the Nutella! You should use at least ¾ cup.) Wet the edge, all the way around with water. Fold the top over and press the edges together to seal. You can cut closely around the edge to seal.

If serving to company, roll leftover dough into a long narrow strip. Cut 3 equal half-inch strips. Braid the strips together to make a long braid. Wet the edge of the calzone with water. Arrange the braid around the edge of the calzone and press it down lightly.

Brush with milk and bake for 6–8 minutes. Sprinkle with powdered sugar and cut into strips. Garnish with berries and whipped cream if desired, or just eat plain. Best eaten while warm so the Nutella oozes out!

Makes 6 slices.

Oatmeal Honey Scotchies

1 cup butter
¾ cup brown sugar
½ cup honey
2 eggs
1 teaspoon vanilla
½ teaspoon cinnamon
1 teaspoon baking soda
½ teaspoon salt
3 cups rolled or quick oats
1 ½ cups flour*
1 11-ounce package butterscotch-flavored chips

Preheat oven to 375°.

In a medium sized bowl, cream butter, brown sugar, and honey together. Add eggs and vanilla and mix well. Add cinnamon, baking soda, salt, and mix together. Add oats, flour, and butterscotch chips, and mix together, scraping down the sides of the bowl until just combined.

Drop by tablespoons onto an ungreased baking sheet and bake for 8–10 minutes for soft cookies or 10–12 for crisp cookies. Cool for 5 minutes and remove to a cooling rack with a spatula.

Makes about 4 dozen cookies.

*For a lower altitude, 1 ¼ cup of flour may be sufficient.

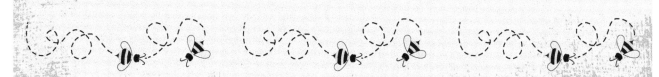

Banana Cupcakes with Honey Cinnamon Frosting

1 ½ cups flour
1 teaspoon baking powder
½ teaspoon baking soda
¼ teaspoon salt
¾ cup sugar
½ cup butter, melted
1 ½ cups mashed banana (4–5 bananas)
2 large eggs
½ teaspoon vanilla

Preheat oven to 350° and prepare 24 muffin tins with cupcake liners.

In a small bowl, mix flour, baking powder, baking soda, and salt. Stir to combine and set aside. In a medium bowl, cream sugar, butter, and mashed bananas. Add eggs and vanilla and mix well. Incorporate dry ingredients and mix together until smooth. Do not over mix.

Fill cupcake liners two-thirds of the way full and bake 18–20 minutes or until they spring back to the touch. Let cool completely and frost with honey cinnamon frosting.

Makes 18 cupcakes.

Honey Cinnamon Frosting
½ cup butter, softened
1 ½ cups powdered sugar
1 tablespoon honey
¼ teaspoon ground cinnamon

Cream butter until fluffy. Add powdered sugar, honey, and cinnamon and mix until light and creamy. (Add milk by the teaspoon if necessary, until desired consistency.)

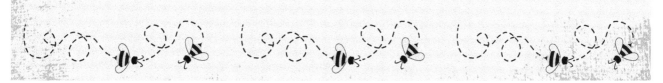

Peanut Butter and Honey Powerballs

½ cup peanut butter
¼ cup honey
½ teaspoon vanilla
Dash of salt
⅓ cup vanilla or chocolate protein powder*
¾ cup rolled oats

Mix peanut butter, honey, vanilla, and salt together. Add protein powder and stir. Add oats and mix until combined. Using a cookie scoop, scoop dough into bite-sized balls and store in the refrigerator until ready to eat.

*You can substitute ¼ cup powdered milk.

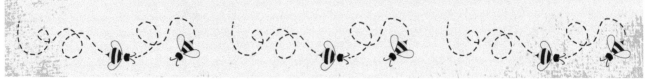

Honey Crunch Popcorn

1 cup honey
½ cup sugar
2 tablespoons butter
½ teaspoon salt
½ teaspoon baking soda

Boil honey and sugar on low and cook until hard ball stage* or 250°. Take off heat and stir in butter until dissolved. Add baking soda and stir well. Pour over 3–4 cups popped popcorn. Stir mixture throughout and cool. Break into pieces.

*If you don't have a candy thermometer, place a cup of ice water by the stove. Let honey and sugar mixture come to a boil and boil gently for 3 minutes. Drop a teaspoon of the mixture into the ice water. The mixture is ready when the drop forms a firm ball that keeps its shape. It should not crack in water.

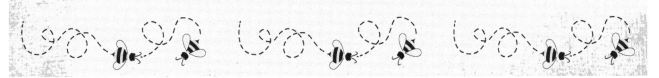

Bienenstich Cake

Cake

1 ¼ teaspoons active dry yeast
¾ cup whole milk, warmed just over room temperature with
1 tablespoon raw honey added
¼ cup sugar
1 cup bread flour
1 cup all-purpose flour
¾ teaspoon salt
2 large eggs, at room temperature
4 tablespoons unsalted butter, at room temperature

Combine the yeast and milk with honey and let sit for five minutes.
Cream the butter and sugar in a medium mixing bowl. Add the yeast mixture to the butter mixture, and mix until combined. Add all other cake ingredients to this mixture. This is thick, like dough, so if you are not Amish and you use electricity, you can mix this together in a stand mixer at low-medium speed for 2 to 3 minutes. If you are Amish, you've just got to use your muscles. (We often ask Poppy to do this part.) Add eggs and mix. Scrape down the sides of the bowl, cover with plastic wrap, and let rise in a warm place for 60 minutes until the dough is a little puffy. It won't fully double.

Butter a 9-inch round spring form pan. Stir the batter a few times to deflate it slightly, then scrape it into the prepared pan and spread it until it fills the bottom. Cover with plastic wrap (don't let the plastic sag and touch the dough) and let it rise for another 30 minutes.
Preheat oven to 350°.

Honey Almond Topping

9 tablespoons unsalted butter
⅓ cup plus 3 tablespoons granulated sugar
4 ½ tablespoons honey
3 tablespoons heavy cream
1 ½ cups sliced almonds
3 pinches of sea salt

In a small or medium saucepan, stir butter, sugar, honey, cream, and salt over medium heat until butter is melted. Stirring frequently, bring to a simmer and let boil for 3 to 5 minutes, until the mixture goes from a yellowish color to a light beige. Remove from heat and stir in the almonds.

(Continued) Bienenstich Cake

Once the cake has finished its second rise—remember that it won't rise significantly—press the dough lightly to deflate it. Spoon the almond topping evenly over the top of the cake.

Bake cake for 20 to 25 minutes until the top is a lovely golden-brown color and a toothpick inserted in the center comes out clean. Be sure to put a foil-lined cookie sheet under your spring form pan in case the almond topping drips.

Transfer to a cooling rack and let it sit in the pan for 10 minutes. After 10 minutes, run a knife between the cake and the pan and remove the outer ring. Let cool completely.

Pastry Cream Filling

1 cup whole milk
1 teaspoon pure vanilla extract or ¼ teaspoon almond extract (we use almond)
3 large egg yolks
¼ cup granulated sugar
3 tablespoons all-purpose flour
2 pinches sea salt
2 tablespoons unsalted butter, softened

Warm milk in a medium saucepan (not too warm or it will scald). Set aside. Rinse saucepan with cool water and dry it. In the cool saucepan, whisk the egg yolks and sugar for 1 minute. Whisk in flour and salt until smooth. Drizzle in warm milk a spoonful at a time while whisking continuously. Once you add half of the milk, you can add the rest in a steady stream, whisking continuously. Return the saucepan to the stove and cook on medium-high heat until the mixture bubbles. Keep whisking, and simmer for 1 to 2 minutes.

Remove from heat and whisk in the butter and either the vanilla or almond extract. Cool the pastry cream completely—either in the fridge or over a bowl of ice water.

To assemble the cake: Once both the cake and pastry cream are cooled, place the cake on a serving platter and cut it horizontally into two layers with a serrated knife. Spread pastry cream over bottom half of the cake. Place the top half of the cake on top of the pastry cream.

You can make the dough and pastry cream a day ahead and refrigerate it. It's quite a bit to do in one day.

 # Sweet as Honey

What's all the buzz about? Find out in this sneak peak of _Sweet as Honey_.

Dan Kanagy stopped his open-air buggy in the middle of the deserted road and turned on his flashlight. Shining it along the roadside, he squinted into the darkness.

There it was. The sign that marked the turnoff to the lane he was looking for, a big, white board decorated with flowers in every variety of paint color imaginable. In bold, black letters it read: BEWARE THE HONEYBEES.

Dan had never been able to figure out if that warning referred to the large number of hives that dotted the Christner's farm or if it referred to the Christners themselves. The community had nicknamed them the Honeybee Sisters a dozen years ago. The three Honeybee _schwesters_ were pretty enough and smart enough to be intimidating, and they lived with their aunt, who was said to be slightly odd. At least that's what Dan had been told. He'd never met the aunt, the _aendi_, but he knew the Honeybee _schwesters_ well. He'd gone to primary school with all three of them.

The youngest, Rose, had seemed so delicate that Dan had feared she'd break if he looked at her the wrong way. Poppy Christner had punched him in the mouth on more than one occasion, and the eldest, Lily, was too wonderful for words, and entirely too wonderful for a plain, ordinary boy like Dan Kanagy.

Beware the Honeybees indeed.

Holding the reins with one hand and the flashlight in the other, Dan turned his horse Clyde down the long lane. It was a good thing he had his flashlight. At two o'clock in the morning under a new

moon in late May, the darkness was profound. Clyde's hooves clip-clopped over a small wooden bridge just wide enough for a buggy or a car to pass over. The light of his flashlight reflected off a pond of still water meandering under the bridge. Maybe *pond* was too generous. It looked more the size of a puddle.

Across the bridge, the lane curved to the right. A variety of tall and short bushes lined the lane to his right, some thick with leaves, others abloom with flowers. To his left, he could just make out a row of beehives, standing guard over the farm.

The line of bushes came to an abrupt stop as he got to the end of the lane. To his left, a small barn loomed above him. A house stood to his right fronted by a lawn full of dandelions and a wide flower bed bursting with blooms. Even by the light of his flashlight, they looked wonderful-*gute*. The bees probably thought they were wonderful-*gute* too.

Dan jumped out of his buggy and tiptoed up the path of flagstones that led to the house, not sure why he tried to be quiet. He was about to awaken the whole house. It couldn't be helped, but he still felt bad about interrupting their sleep like this.

He walked up the porch steps, tapped lightly on the door, and listened. Nothing.

If he wanted anyone to wake up, he'd have to give up trying to be subtle. He rapped his knuckles five times against the sturdy wooden door. Holding his breath, he listened for signs of movement from within. After a few seconds, a faint light appeared behind the front window curtains. The door slowly creaked open, and Dan found himself nose to nose with the barrel of a shotgun.

He should have paid more heed to that sign.

About The Authors

Jennifer Beckstrand is the award winning Amish romance author of The Matchmakers of Huckleberry Hill series. Her much-anticipated Amish series, *The Honeybee Sisters*, promises to create a lot of romantic buzz. Jennifer has always been drawn to the strong faith and the enduring family ties of the Plain people and loves writing about the antics of Anna and Felty Helmuth and the Honeybee Sisters' *aendi* Bitsy. Jennifer has a degree in mathematics and a passion for Jane Austen and Shakespeare. She and her husband have been married for thirty-two years, and she has four daughters, two sons, and four grandchildren, whom she spoils rotten.

Tearsa Nelson Daines is the oldest daughter of nine children. She learned her culinary skills from her mother who taught her to cook at a very young age. Because of her large family, Tearsa has cooked for many life celebrations that include food. She loves the creative process of cooking and how food is a natural way to bond as a family. She likes to cook for her husband, Brent, alongside her five daughters and two sons, who keep her current with new recipes and food blogs. When not cooking, Tearsa likes to read, travel, plant flowers, go on walks, and waterski, and most of all, spend time with her husband, seven children, three sons-in-law, five grandchildren, extended family, and friends.

Alicia Johnson loves to take an empty space and fill it with people and things to create a memory. Because of this, she has always loved taking pictures. Alicia is a wife and a mother of four beautiful and talented children. She enjoys taking trips with her family and watching her children do the things they love. Alicia loves to design and sew because fabrics and textures have the power to change moods and make all the difference in a home. She also loves to cook for her family, particularly that which satisfies their collective sweet tooth. There are few things that a big hug or good piece of chocolate can't fix.

CPSIA information can be obtained
at www.ICGtesting.com
Printed in the USA
LVHW072310120619
621066LV00017B/172/P

9 780997 699302